**Lower**

# EARLY LITERACY GAMES

## PLAY TO LEARN

GW00729020

Little Jack Horner
Sat in the corner
Eating a Christmas pie
He put in his thumb
And pulled out a plum
And said, 'What a good boy am I'

**Lots and lots
of fun games**

Written by Christine Gallacher and Margaret Grubb
Published by Prim-Ed Publishing

# Early Literacy Games

## Foreword

*Early Literacy Games* is a book of games designed to consolidate and reinforce early literacy skills in the areas of rhyming, phonics, word building and sight vocabulary.

The games have a variety of functions. They help to develop:

- phonological awareness;
- listening skills; and
- concentration skills.

In the wider concept they encourage:

- cooperation learning (taking turns etc); and
- the development of communication skills (explaining rules etc).

It is important when building the foundation of a pupil's reading that he or she experiences success, satisfaction, independence and active involvement. By providing the media of games in *Early Literacy Games*, teachers, parents and peers can work with the pupil in contributing to this learning process.

Books in this series are: *Early Literacy Games (Lower)*
*Literacy Games (Lower – Middle)*

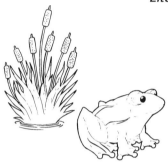

## Contents

## Explanation of Terms Used

### ♦ Phonological Awareness

This is the awareness of the sounds in spoken words. Pupils develop the ability to attend and segment words into 'chunks' of sound – phonemes (the smallest units), syllables, onset/rime etc.

### ♦ Onset/Rime

These are the separate sounds in a word. The beginning of the word is the onset and the rest of the word is the rime. For example c–at. (Note: words that rhyme sound the same at the end because they share a rime. For example c–at, fl–at).

## Using the Games

Each game in the book has a photocopiable:

- set of rules/equipment needed;
- game board; and
- set of words or letter patterns corresponding to the game.

These can be:

- enlarged for class use; or
- copied and coloured for pupils' personal ownership for practise at home with family and friends.

Parents can then be involved with their child's learning in an informal, yet fun, environment.

The games can also be adapted to include words or sounds being covered in the class literacy programme.

Games require a teacher or parent helper to assist with difficulties and help with checking and scoring until proficiency is reached.

## Making the Games

– Game boards photocopied onto stiff card—A4 or preferably enlarged to A3. Coloured by teacher, parent helper or pupils. Laminate for prolonged use.

– Photocopy rules page for each game. The rules could be glued on the back of the game board for future reference.

– Collect sets of coloured counters, buttons etc. Sets of six different colours are needed for some games, while others need eight or ten different colours repeated in each set.

– Purchase or prepare dice with the following:

- dice with numbers 1, 2 and 3 only;
- dice with sounds squ, ch, sh, wh, th and ing;
- dice with sounds ck, le, oo, nk, y and ea; and
- dice with vowels a, e, i, o, u and * on 6th side.

– Photocopy sets of words and sounds on pages 48–58 onto stiff coloured card or paper and laminate before cutting and sorting into appropriate packs. An alternative is to copy onto blank playing cards. Colour coding helps keep packs from becoming mixed up.
Note: The lists of common words can be replaced with words being dealt with in the class programme such as topic words or personal words children are having difficulty reading. A blank word card master sheet has been provided on page 61. Blank playing cards could also be used.

– Photocopies of scoresheet on page 60.

# Curriculum Links — England

The activities in *Early Literacy Games* and *Literacy Games* have been written to encourage children to demonstrate the following English and Mathematics Programme of Study objectives from the National Curriculum:

| Subject | Key Stage | Programme of Study |
|---|---|---|
| **English** | **One** | • *Speaking and Listening:*<br>2a. Listen with sustained concentration<br>2b. Remember specific points<br>9b. Listen to adults giving detailed explanations and presentations |
| | | • *Reading:*<br>1a.  Hear, identify, segment and blend phonemes in words<br>1c.  Link sound and letter patterns, exploring rhyme, and other sound patterns<br>1f.  Read on sight high-frequency words and other familiar words<br>1g.  Recognise words with common spelling patterns |
| | | • *Writing:*<br>4b.  Use knowledge of sound-symbol relationships and phonological patterns when spelling<br>4c.  Recognise and use simple spelling patterns<br>4d.  Write common letter strings<br>4e.  Spell common words |
| **Maths** | **One** | • *Number:*<br>2a.  Count reliably up to 20 objects |
| | | • *Shape, Space and Measures:*<br>3b.  Recognise movements in a straight line |
| **English** | **Two** | • *Reading:*<br>1a.  Use phonemic awareness and phonic knowledge<br>1b.  Use word recognition and graphic knowledge |
| | | • *Writing:*<br>4c.  Apply knowledge of spelling conventions<br>4d.  Use knowledge of common letter strings and visual patterns<br>4f.  Revise and build on their knowledge of words and spelling patterns<br>4i.  Relevance of word families |

The activities in *Early Literacy Games and Literacy Games* have been written to encourage children to demonstrate the following English and Mathematics objectives from the 5-14 Curriculum:

| Subject | Strand | Level | | |
|---------|--------|:---:|:---:|:---:|
| | | **A** | **B** | **C** |
| **English** | *Listening:* | | | |
| | Listening for information, instructions and directions | • | • | • |
| | Listening in groups | • | • | |
| | Knowledge about language | | • | |
| | *Talking:* | | | |
| | Conveying information, instructions and directions | • | • | • |
| | Talking in groups | • | • | • |
| | Audience awareness | • | • | • |
| | *Reading:* | | | |
| | Reading for information | • | | |
| | *Writing:* | | | |
| | Functional writing | • | • | |
| | Spelling | • | | |
| | Handwriting and presentation | • | | |
| **Maths** | *Number, money and measurement:* | | | |
| | Range and type of numbers | • | | |
| | *Shape, position and movement:* | | | |
| | Position and movement | • | | |

# Rhyme and Match

♦ **Aim**

To practise and consolidate listening skills in the detection of rhyme. It is most important that the players find it to be a positive and enjoyable experience. This promotes self-esteem.

♦ **Equipment Needed**

- Boxes of eight and ten sets of coloured counters or buttons.
- Select appropriate level of game.
- Sets A, B and C have eight pictures per card. Sets D and E have ten.

♦ **How to Play**

- Number of players – 2.

- Each player receives one of the rhyme and match game boards from the same set.

- First player selects a coloured counter and places it on one of the pictures on his/her board.

- That player calls out the name of the picture and asks the second player to put a similar-coloured counter on the rhyming picture on his/her board.

- It is now the second player's turn to select a counter and place it on a picture.

- The game continues until all pictures are covered.

- Corresponding rhyming pictures are checked. Helper can assist if necessary.

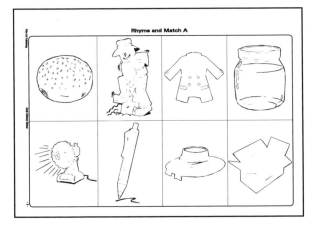

♦ **For the Helper**

Set A – bun/sun, dig/pig, coat/goat, jar/car, fan/pan, pen/ten, hat/cat, box/fox

Set B – chest/nest, lock/clock, trunk/sunk, bread/bed, sack/crack, ship/zip, sing/string, hutch/crutch

Set C – dog/log, cot/pot, train/rain, stitch/switch, snail/nail, house/mouse, rake/cake, ball/wall

Set D – brick/kick, king/ring, sky/fly, path/bath, oil/boil, stew/screw, chips/lips, sink/wink, moon/balloon, toe/bow

Set E – boy/toy, wing/swing, tray/spray, ant/plant, tube/cube, rock/sock, fish/dish, handle/candle, cook/book, sleep/sheep

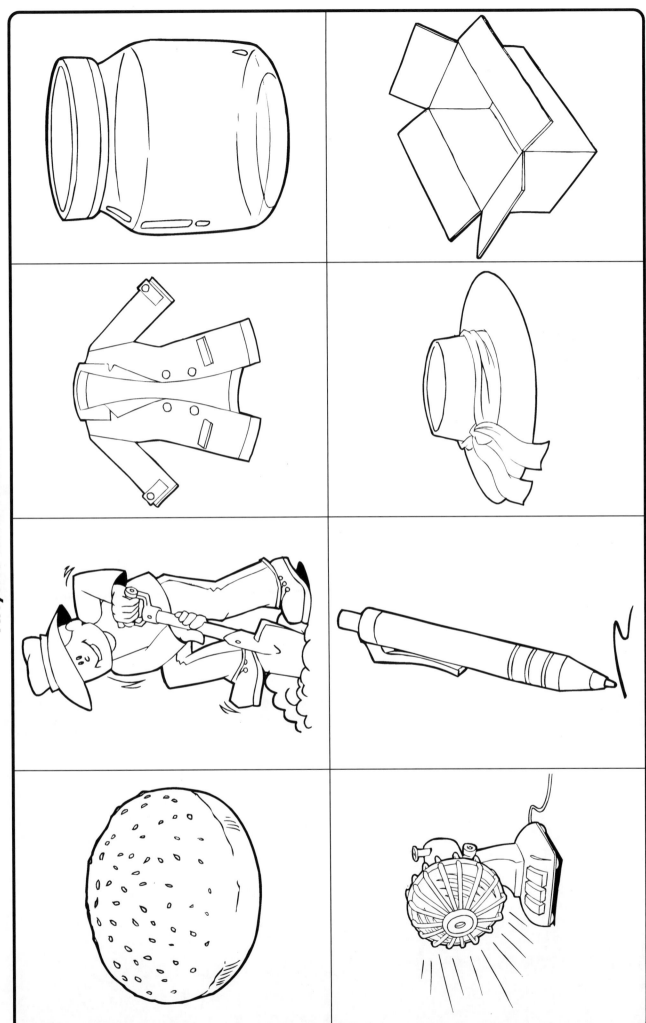

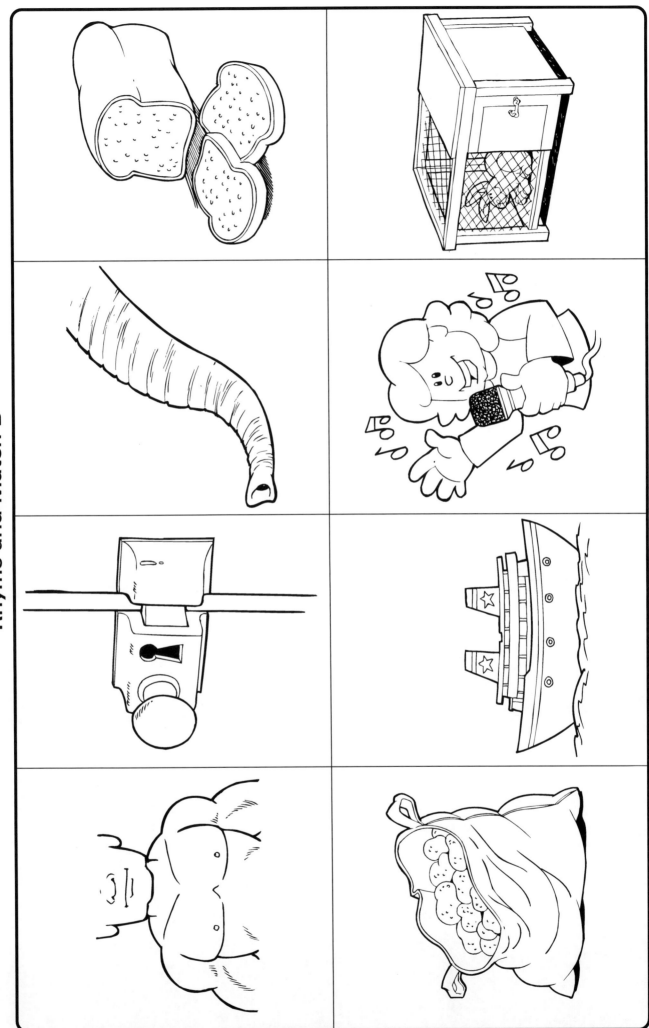

*Early Literacy Games*

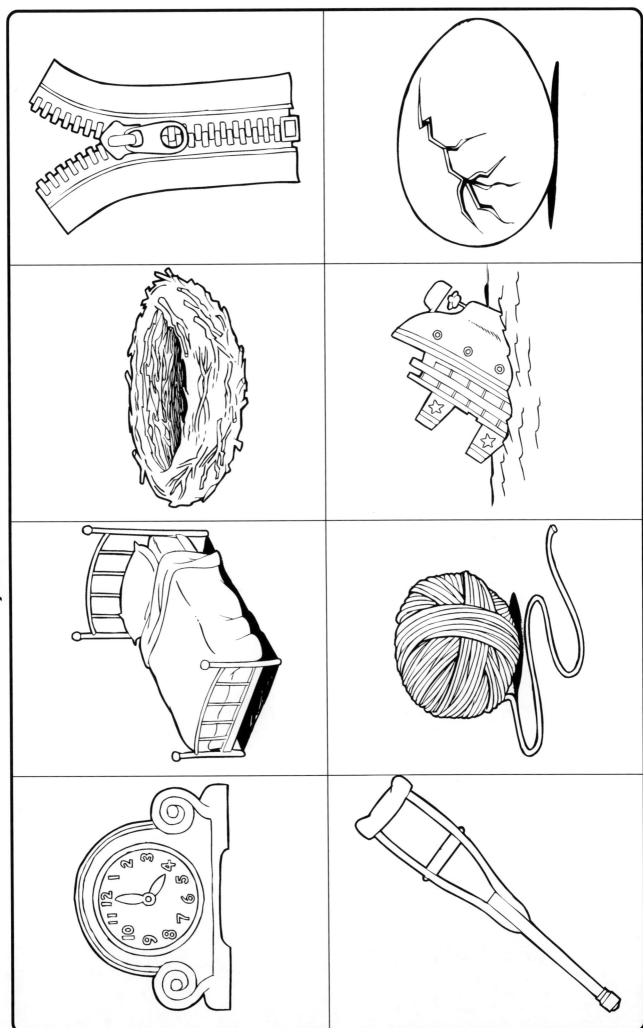

Rhyme and Match B

*Early Literacy Games*

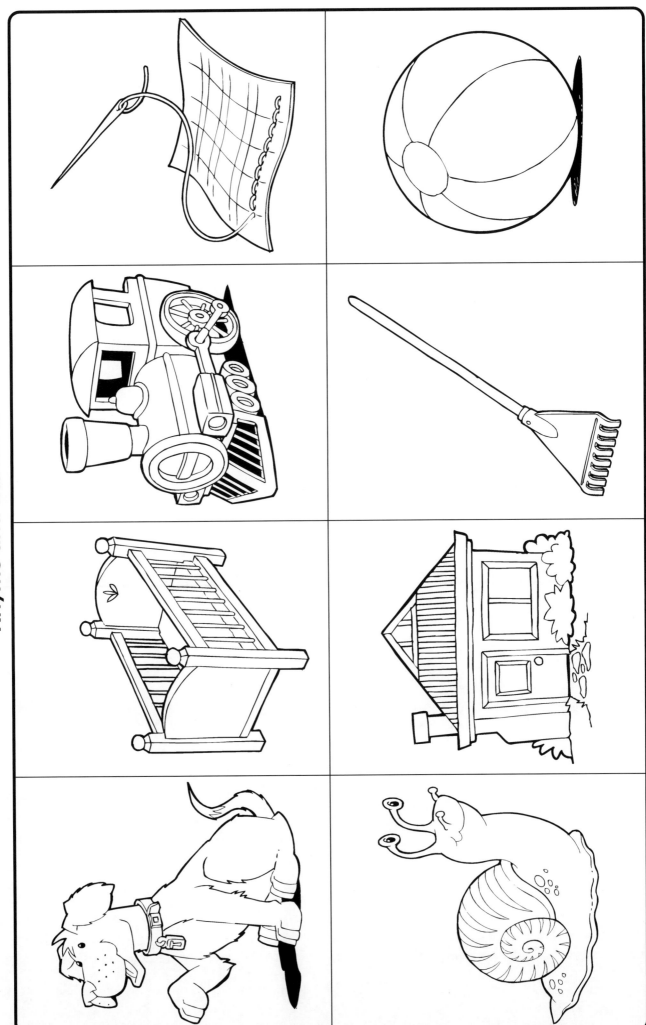

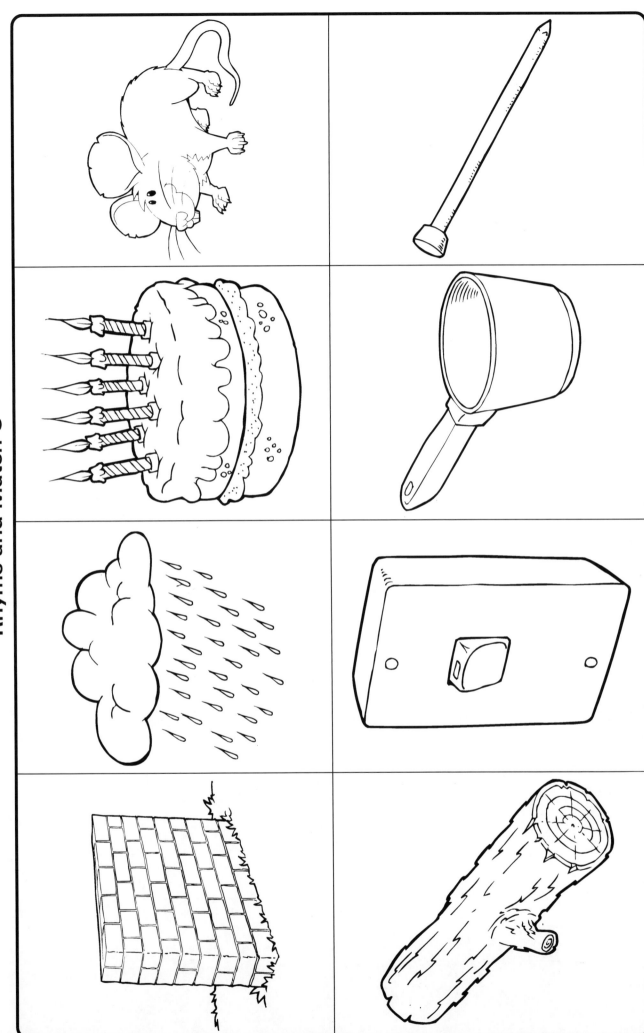

*Early Literacy Games*

*Early Literacy Games*

# Rhyme and Match E

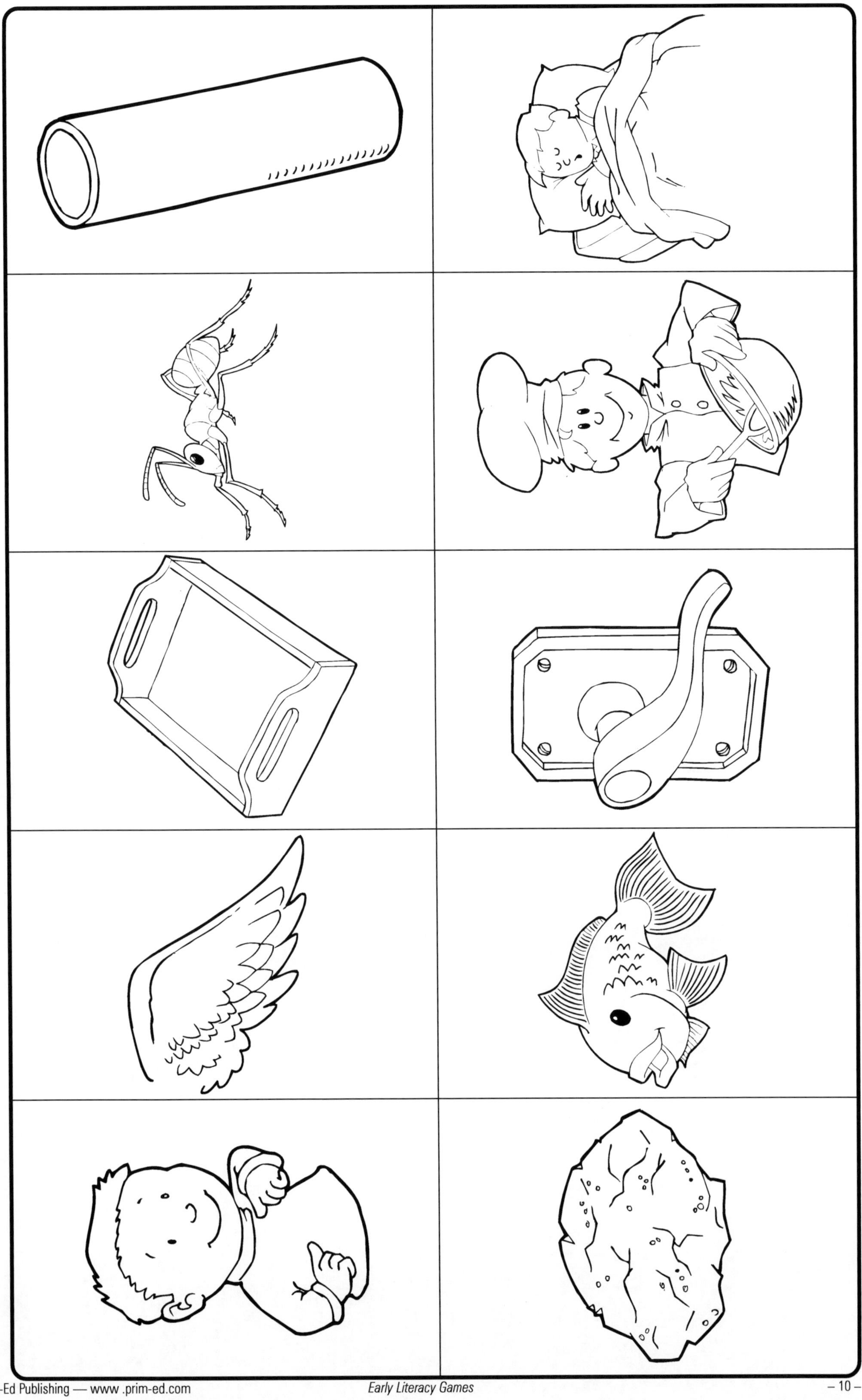

*Early Literacy Games*

♦ *Aim*

To practise and consolidate rhyming skills. It is important that the players find it to be a positive and enjoyable experience. This promotes self-esteem.

♦ *Equipment Needed*

- Die numbered with 1, 2 and 3 only.
- Different coloured counter for each player.
- Plum Rhymes game board A or B.

♦ *How To Play*

- Number of players – 2 or 3.

- Players place his/her counter on Little Jack Horner.

- The first player throws the die and moves his/her counter the corresponding number of places on the game board, landing on a plum.

- The player says as many words as he/she can think of to rhyme with the picture. (Help must be given if they struggle to find a rhyming word).

- The die is then passed to the next player and the game continues until each player reaches the pie at the end of the 'plum tree'.

**Plum Rhymes – A**

Prim-Ed Publishing

Early Literacy Games

Little Jack Horner
Sat in the corner
Eating a Christmas pie
He put in his thumb
And pulled out a plum
And said, 'What a good boy am I!'

– 13 –

Little Jack Horner
Sat in the corner
Eating a Christmas pie
He put in his thumb
And pulled out a plum
And said, 'What a good boy am I!'

Little Jack Horner

Sat in the corner

Eating a Christmas pie

He put in his thumb

And pulled out a plum

And said, 'What a good boy am I!'

*Early Literacy Games*

The game board for One, Two, Three, Four, Five can be played in two different ways.

### ◆ Aim (Game A)

To practise and consolidate word building using onset and rime.

### ◆ Aim (Game B)

To practise and consolidate word building using sound blends.

It is important that the players find it to be a positive and enjoyable experience. This promotes self-esteem.

### ◆ Equipment Needed

- Die with numbers 1 – 6.
- Different coloured counter for each player.
- One, Two, Three, Four, Five game board.
- Two packs of cards – Game A – Onset and Rime packs
  - Game B – Beginnings and Endings packs

(These items can be found in the Word Lists and Sounds section at the end of the book.)

- Scoresheet and pencil

### ◆ How to Play

- Number of players – 2 or 3.

  Game A: place Onset cards face down on the net (marked 1) and Rime cards on the treasure chest (marked 2).

  Game B: place Beginnings cards face down on the net (marked 1) and Endings packs on the treasure chest (marked 2).

- Players place his/her counter on any fish to start.

- First player throws the die and moves his/her counter clockwise according to the number on the die.

- If he/she lands on a fish marked 1 they collect a card from the net; if on a fish marked 2 a card from the treasure chest. Next player has a turn.

- As cards from each pack are collected he/she will be able to make actual words.

- Words are written on the scoresheet under his/her name.

- Cards can be used more than once.

- Game continues until helper decides the game is over.

- Players read out the words he/she has made.

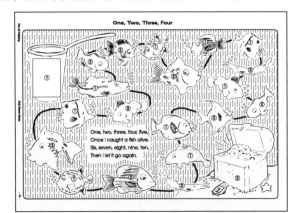

# One, Two, Three, Four, Five

One, two, three, four, five,
Once I caught a fish alive.
Six, seven, eight, nine, ten.
Then I let it go again.

# Frog on a Log

The game board for Frog on a Log can be played in two different ways.

### ♦ *Aim (Game A)*

To practise and consolidate word building using onset and rime.

### ♦ *Aim (Game B)*

To practise and consolidate word building using sound blends.

It is important that the players find it to be a positive and enjoyable experience. This promotes self-esteem.

### ♦ *Equipment Needed*

- Die with numbers 1 – 6.
- Different coloured counter for each player.
- Frog on a Log game board.
- Two packs of cards – Game A – Onset and Rime packs.
  - Game B – Beginnings and Endings packs.
  (These items can be found in the Word Lists and Sounds section at the end of the book.)
- Scoresheet and pencil

### ♦ *How to Play*

- Number of players – 2 or 3.

- Game A – Place Onset cards face down on the large lilypad without a flower and Rime cards on the large lilypad with a flower.

- Game B – Place Beginnings cards face down on the large lilypad without a flower and Endings packs on the large lilypad with a flower.

- Players place his/her counter on Froggy.

- First player throws the die and moves his/her counter according to the number on the die.

- If he/she lands on a lilypad without a flower they collect a card from the corresponding lilypad; if on a flowered lilypad the same applies. Next player has a turn.

- As cards from each pack are collected he/she will be able to make actual words. Words are written on the scoresheet under his/her name.

- Cards can be used more than once.

- Game continues until helper decides the game is over.

- Players read out the words he/she has made.

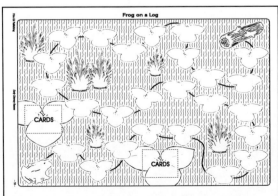

Frog on a Log

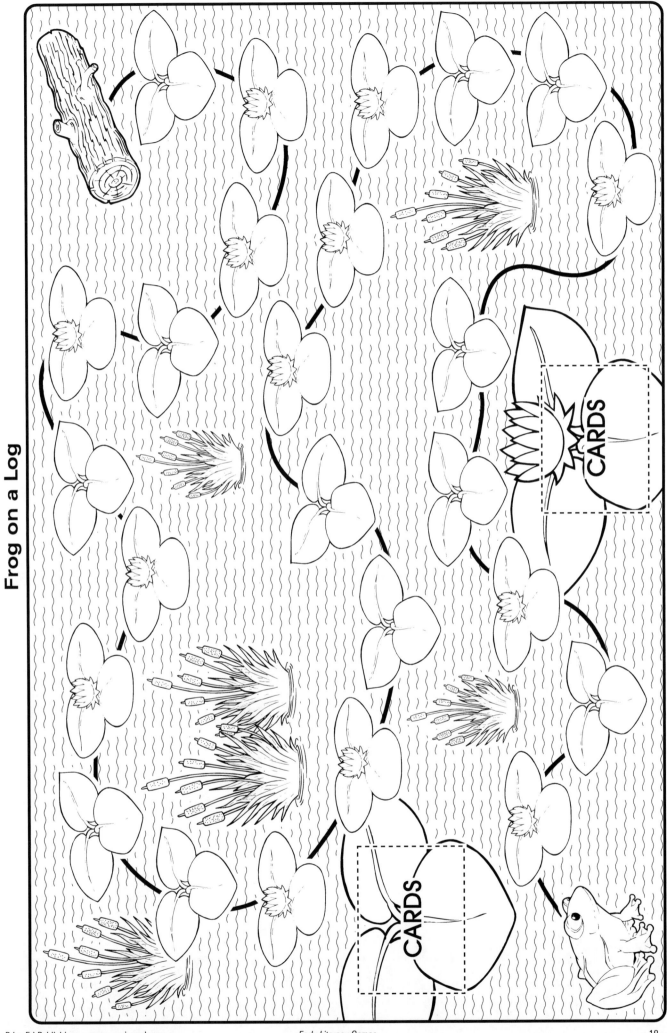

*Early Literacy Games*

# Hat Trick

The game board for Hat Trick can be played in two different ways.

## ♦ *Aim (Game A)*

To practise and consolidate word building using onset and rime.

## ♦ *Aim (Game B)*

To practise and consolidate word building using sound blends.

It is important that the players find it to be a positive and enjoyable experience. This promotes self-esteem.

## ♦ *Equipment Needed*

- Die with numbers 1 – 6.
- Different coloured counter for each player.
- Hat Trick game board.
- Two packs of cards – Game A – Onset and Rime packs.
    Game B – Beginnings and Endings packs.
  (These items can be found in the Word Lists and Sounds section at the end of the book.)
- Scoresheet and pencil

## ♦ *How to Play*

- Number of players – 2 or 3.

- Game A – Place Onset cards face down on Teg, the alien and Rime cards on Zog, the alien.

- Game B – Place Beginnings cards face down on Teg, the alien and Endings packs on Zog, the alien.

- Players place his/her counter on any hat with a letter on to start.

- First player throws the die and moves his/her counter clockwise according to the number on the die, helping Teg and Zog to try on the hats.

- If he/she lands on a hat with a 'T' they collect a card from Teg. If they land on a hat with a 'Z' they collect a card from Zog.

- Next player has a turn.

- As cards from each pack are collected, he/she will be able to make actual words. Words are written on the scoresheet under his/her name. Cards can be used more than once.

- Game continues until helper decides the game is over.

- Players read out the words he/she has made.

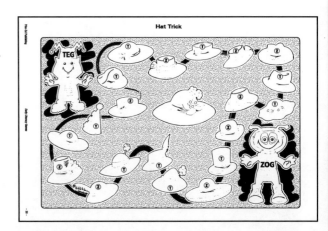

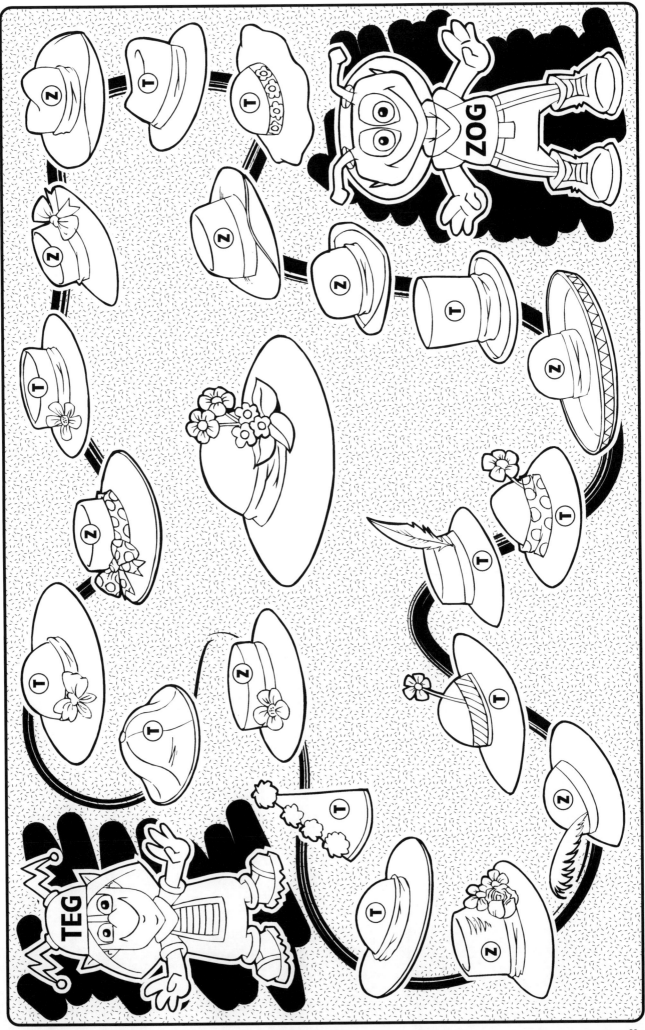

*Early Literacy Games*

♦ **Aim**

Games A and B – To practise and consolidate phonic skills. It is important that the players find it to be a positive and enjoyable experience. This promotes self-esteem.

♦ **Equipment Needed**

- Die with **sh**, **squ**, **ch**, **wh**, **th**, and **ing** for Game A.
- Die with **ck**, **le**, **oo**, **ea**, **y** and **nk** for Game B.
- Appropriate Sound Trail game board.
- Different coloured counter for each player.

♦ **How to Play**

- Number of players – 2 or 3

- The first player throws the die and moves forwards to the next picture containing that sound. However, on route to that picture he/she must say the sound in each picture (as shown on the castle) along the way. For example; A **ch**, is thrown. Player says **sh** as in fi**sh**, **wh** as in **wh**eel and **ch** as in **ch**air.

- Help must be given if player struggles with the sounds. Note: words with sounds are shown below to assist the helper.

- Next player has a turn and the game continues until all players reach the castle at the end of the sound trail.

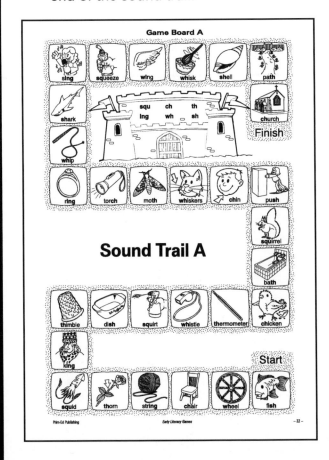

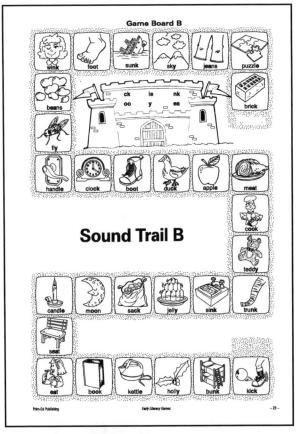

Note: oo says o͞o (moon)
o̯o (book)
y says ee (holly)
i-e (fly)

# Game Board A

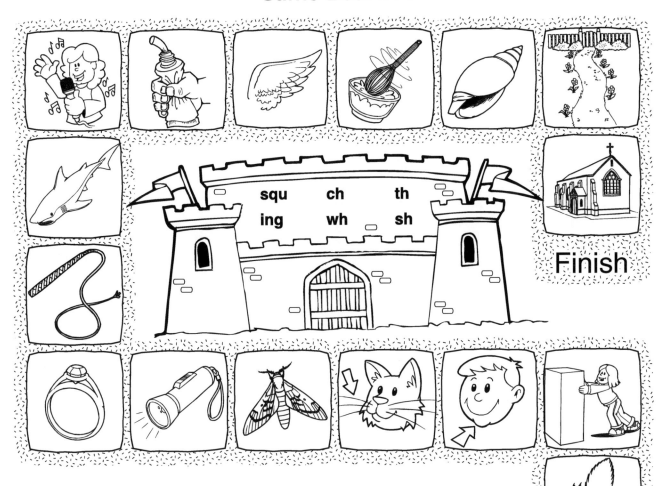

squ    ch    th

ing    wh    sh

Finish

# Sound Trail A

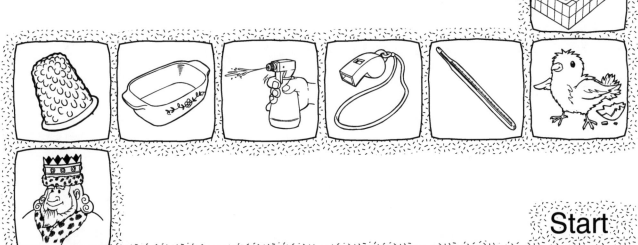

Start

ck    le    nk
oo    y    ea

Finish

# Sound Trail B

Start

### ◆ Aim

Games A and B – To practise and consolidate phonic skills identifying the medial (middle) sound in words. It is important that the players find it to be a positive and enjoyable experience. This promotes self-esteem.

### ◆ Equipment Needed

- Die with, **a, e, i, o, u** and **\*** for games A and B.
- Appropriate sound trail game board.
- Different coloured counter for each player.

### ◆ How to Play

- Number of players – 2 or 3

- The first player throws the die and moves forwards to the next picture containing that sound. However, on route to that picture he/she must say the middle vowel sound in each picture along the way. For example; an **e** is thrown. Player says **a** as in b**a**t, **i** as in w**i**g and **e** as in p**e**n.

- Help must be given if player struggles with the sounds. Note: words with medial vowel sounds are shown below to assist the helper.

- If a player throws a **\*** he/she misses a turn.

- Next player has a turn and the game continues until all players reach the castle at the end of the middle trail.

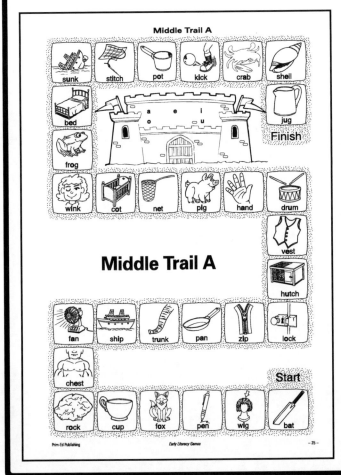

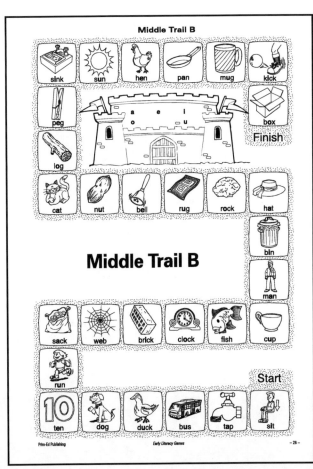

Finish

# Middle Trail A

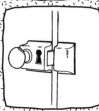

Start

## Middle Trail B

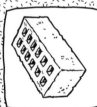

**Start**

# Humpty Dumpty

### ♦ *Aim*

To practise and consolidate sight vocabulary. It is important that the players find it to be a positive and enjoyable experience. This promotes self-esteem.

### ♦ *Equipment Needed*

- Different coloured counter for each player.
- Pack of 25 commonly used words cards.

### ♦ *How to Play*

- Number of players – 1 to 6.

- Pack of word cards placed face down beside game board.

- Players place counters on the start.

- First player picks up a card and reads the word. If he/she cannot read the word, then read the word for them and ask the player to look at the word and repeat it.

- The player then moves counter according to the number indicated on the card.

- Replace card at the bottom of the pack.

- Each player has a turn reading one card at a time until all players reach the top of the wall.

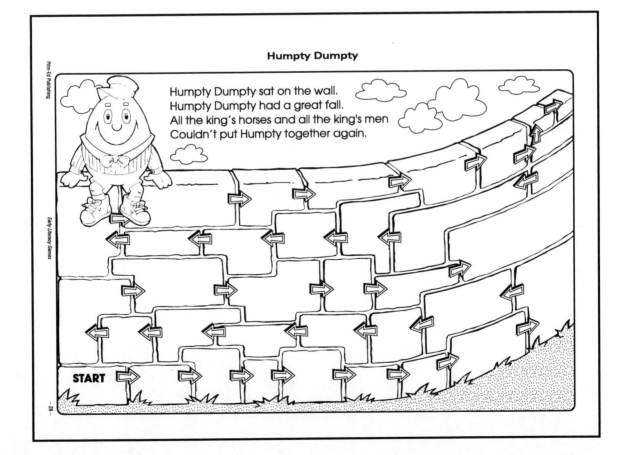

**Humpty Dumpty**

Humpty Dumpty sat on the wall.
Humpty Dumpty had a great fall.
All the king's horses and all the king's men
Couldn't put Humpty together again.

START

# Humpty Dumpty

Humpty Dumpty sat on the wall.
Humpty Dumpty had a great fall.
All the king's horses and all the king's men
Couldn't put Humpty together again.

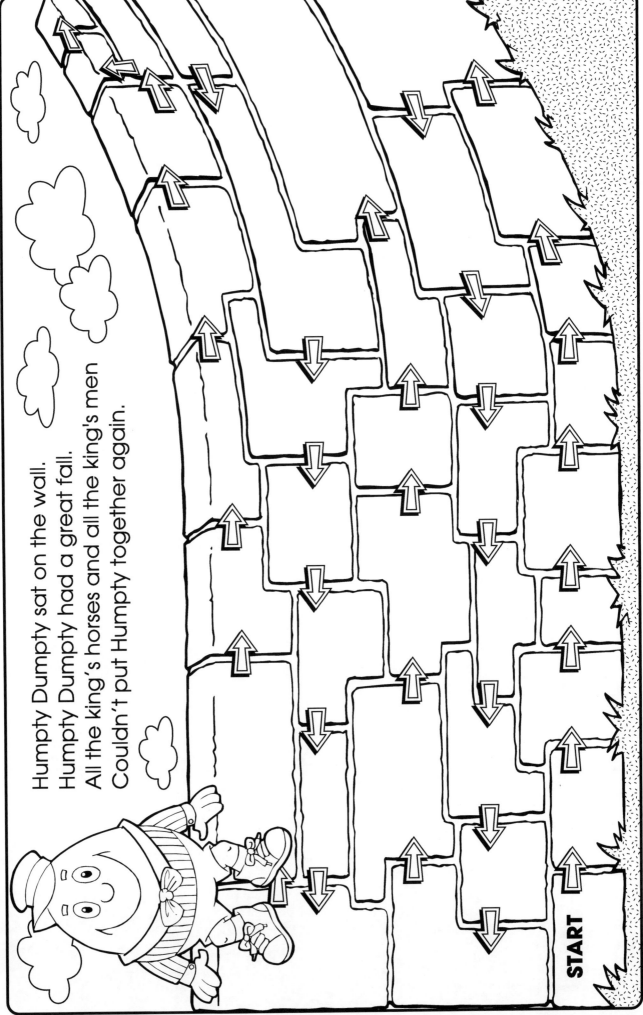

**START**

*Early Literacy Games*

◆ *Aim*

To practise and consolidate sight vocabulary. It is very important that the players find it to be a positive and enjoyable experience. This promotes self-esteem.

◆ *Equipment Needed*

- Different coloured counter for each player.
- Pack of 25 commonly used word cards.

◆ *How to Play*

- Number of players – 1 to 6.

- Pack of word cards placed face down beside game board.

- Players place counters on the start.

- First player picks up a card and reads the word. If he/she cannot read the word, then read the word for them and ask then player to look at the word and repeat it.

- The player then moves counter according to the number indicated on the card.

- Replace at the bottom of the pack.

- Each player has a turn reading one card at a time until all players reach the top of the hill and fetch a pail of water.

Jack and Jill

Jack and Jill went up the hill
To fetch a pail of water.
Jack fell down and broke his crown
And Jill came tumbling after.

FINISH

START

Jack and Jill

Jack and Jill went up the hill
To fetch a pail of water.
Jack fell down and broke his crown
And Jill came tumbling after.

FINISH

START

*Early Literacy Games*

# Goosey, Goosey, Gander

### ♦ *Aim*

To practise and consolidate sight vocabulary. It is important that the players find it to be a positive and enjoyable experience. This promotes self-esteem.

### ♦ *Equipment Needed*

- Different coloured counter for each player.
- Pack of 25 commonly used word cards.

### ♦ *How to Play*

- Number of players – 1 to 6.

- Pack of word cards placed face down beside game board.

- Players place counters on the start.

- First player picks up a card and reads the word. If he/she cannot read the word, then read the word for them and ask the player to look at the word and repeat it.

- The player then moves counter according to the number indicated on the card.

- Replace card at the bottom of the pack.

- Each player has a turn reading one card at a time until all players have moved up and down the stairs.

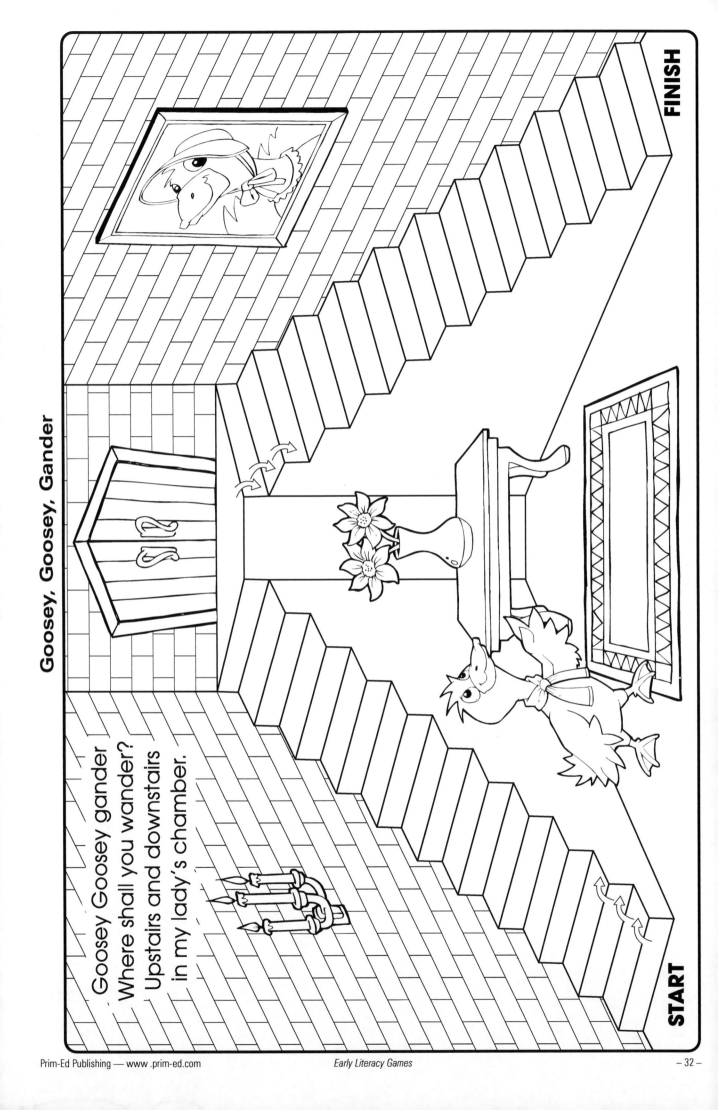

Goosey, Goosey, Gander

Goosey Goosey gander
Where shall you wander?
Upstairs and downstairs
in my lady's chamber.

START

FINISH

# Space Squish!

### ♦ Aim

To practise and consolidate sight vocabulary. It is important that the players find it to be a positive and enjoyable experience. This promotes self-esteem.

### ♦ Equipment Needed

- Die with numbers 1 – 6.
- Four sets of different coloured counters (with four in each set).
- Game board A, B, C or D. (Each game board has different words chosen from the 300 commonly used words list).

### ♦ How to Play

- Number of players – 2 to 4.

- Each player decides which alien pilot they will be – Zog, Teg, Min or Ret. He/she then places his/her four same coloured counters on the spaceships near the alien.

- The aim is to 'fly' each 'spaceship' or counter to the opposite side of the game board.

- The pilots move, in turn, by throwing a die and moving the corresponding number on the die. According to the abilities of the children playing, the pilots could move in different ways:

Level 1 –  Pilots can only move forwards, in straight lines across the board. Pilots may not move backwards, sideways or diagonally.

Level 2 –  Pilots can move forwards, backwards and sideways but not diagonally.

- Along the way there are refuelling stations. The pilots pay for his/her fuel by reading the word. If a pilot cannot read a word, tell them the word and ask them to look at it and repeat it.

- If a pilot lands on an opponent's counter the opponent is 'squished' and sent back to start the journey again.

- More than one spaceship (counter) from each pilot can be 'flying' at the same time.

- The game ends when all pilots safely land all their spaceships on opposite side of the game board.

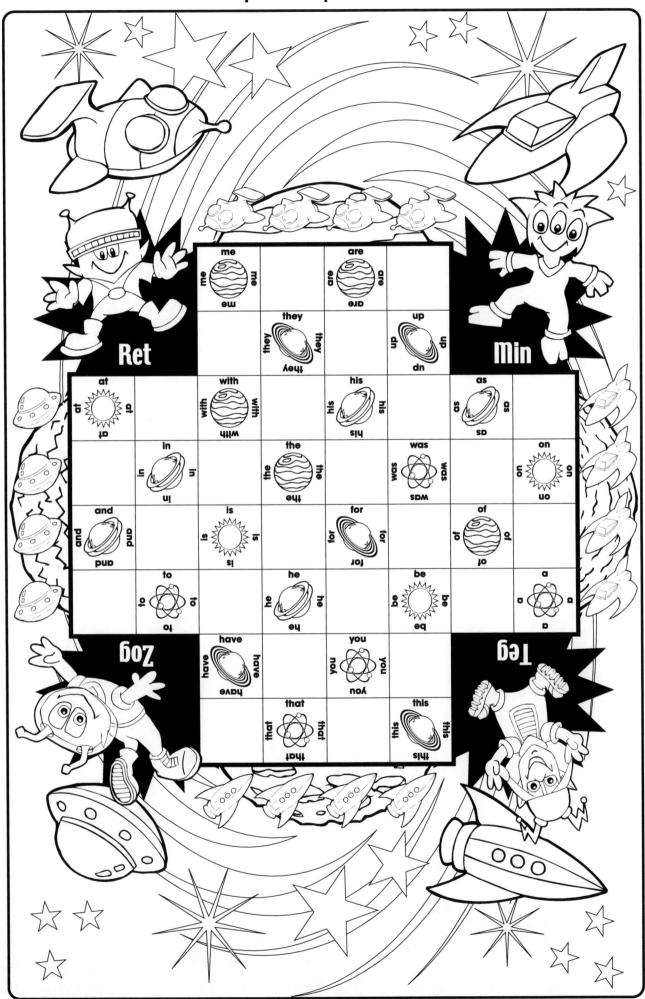

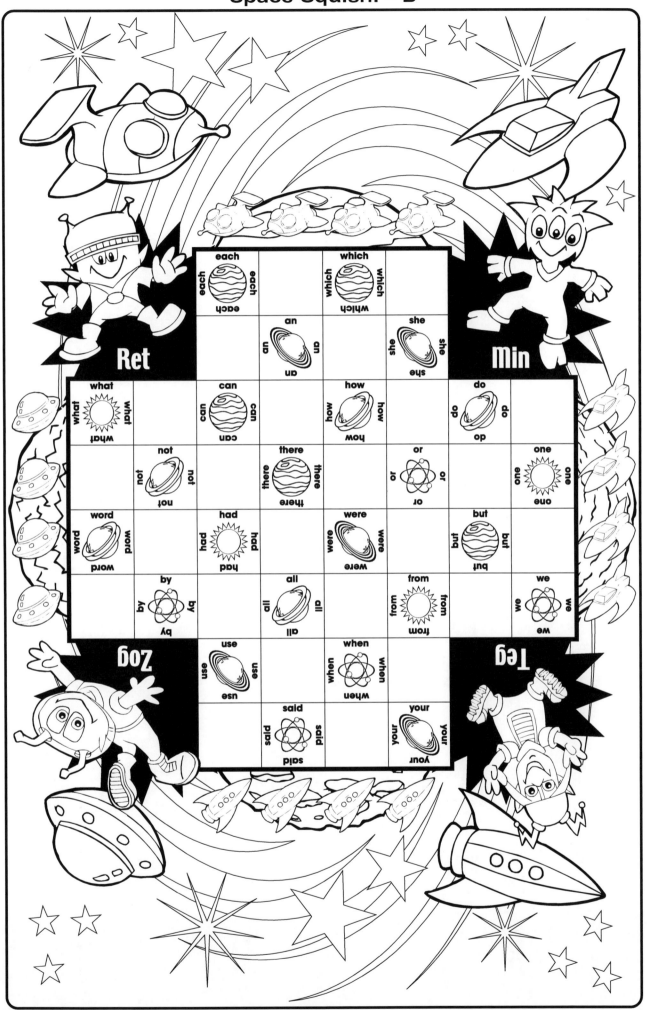

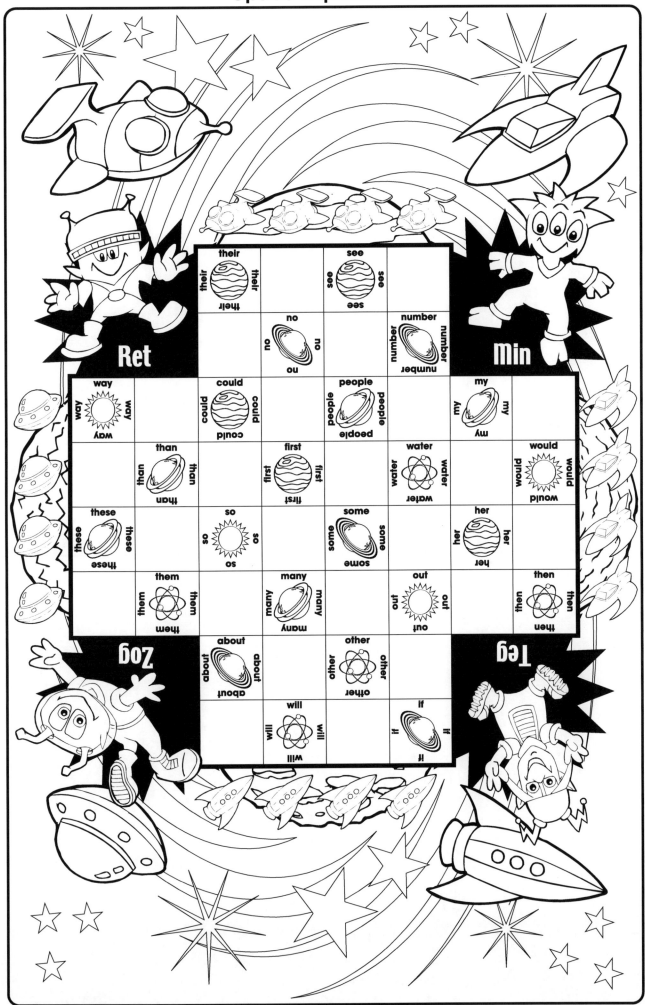

*Early Literacy Games*

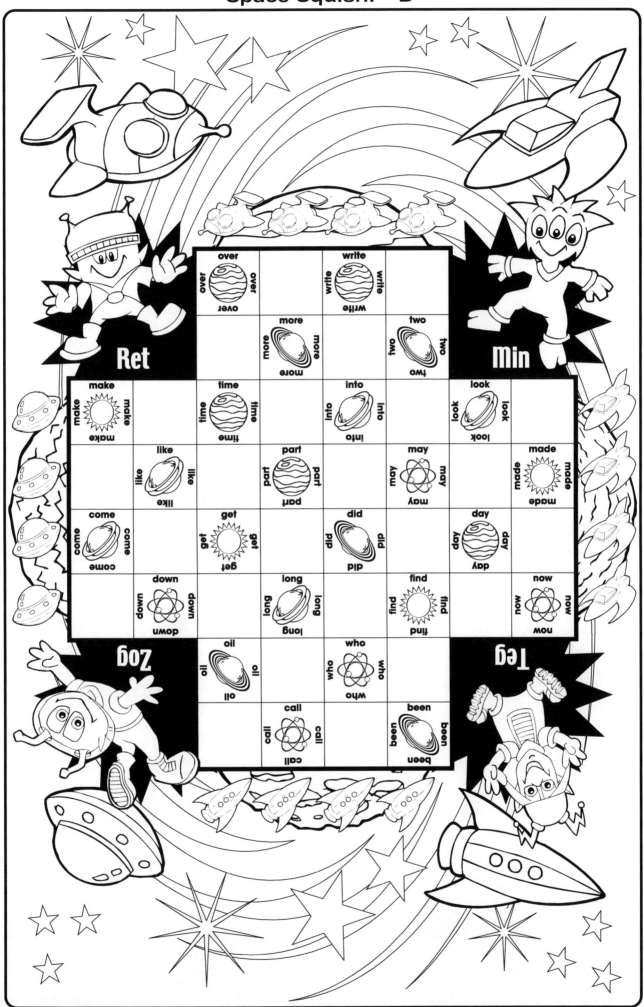

# Sport Squish!

### ♦ Aim

To practise and consolidate sight vocabulary. It is important that the players find it to be a positive and enjoyable experience. This promotes self-esteem.

### ♦ Equipment Needed

- Die with numbers 1 – 6.
- Four sets of different coloured counters (with four in each set).
- Game board A, B, C or D. (Each game board has different words chosen from the 300 commonly used words list.)

### ♦ How to Play

- Number of players – 2 to 4.

- Each player decides which athlete they will be; cricketer, football player, tennis player or basketballer. He/she then places his/her four same coloured counters on the equipment next to the athlete.

- The aim is to get the athlete to the opposite side of the game board.

- The athletes move in turn by throwing a die and moving the corresponding number on the die. According to the abilities of the children playing, the athletes could move in different ways:

Level 1 – Athletes can only move forwards, in straight lines across the board. Athletes may not move backwards, sideways of diagonally.

Level 2 – Athletes can move forwards, backwards and sideways but not diagonally.

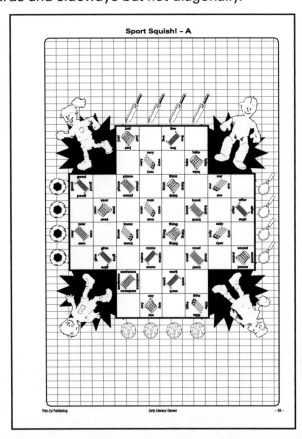

- Along the way there are obstacles to overcome. The athletes overcome these by reading the word. If an athlete cannot read a word, tell them the word and ask them to look at it and repeat it.

- If an athlete lands on an opponent's counter the opponent is 'squished' and sent back to start the journey again.

- More than one counter can be making its way at the same time.

- The game ends when all the athletes reach the opposite side of the gameboard.

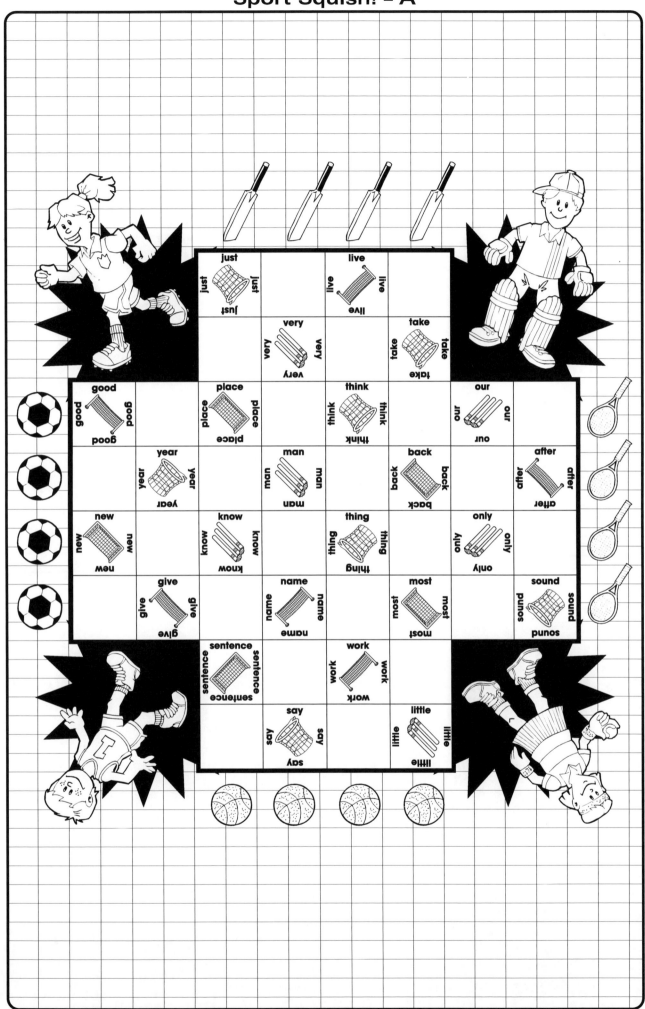

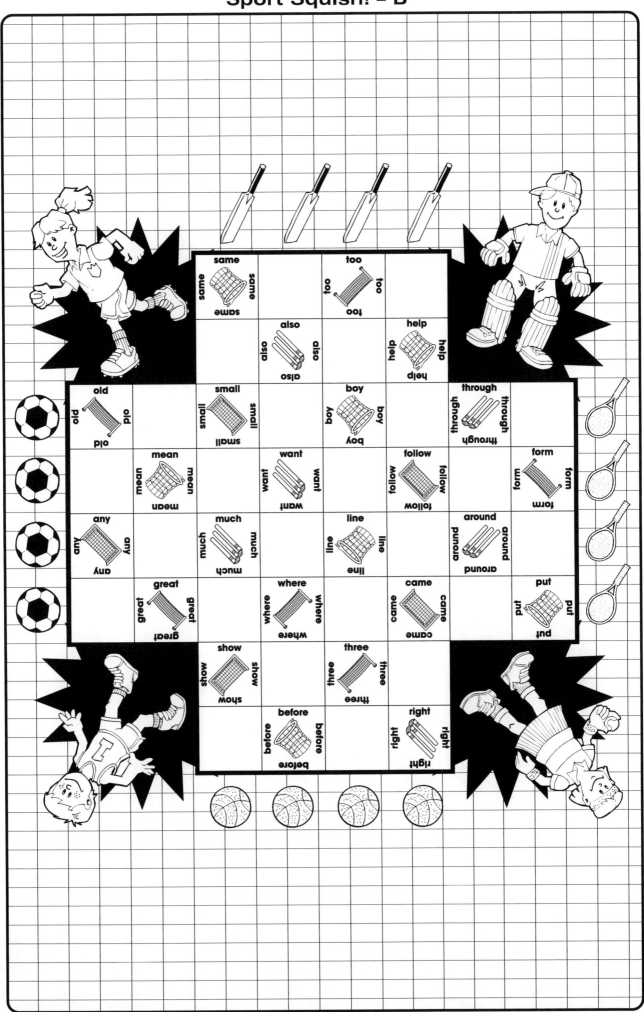

# Sport Squish! – C

| | | | |
|---|---|---|---|
| has | | does | |
| | another | | well |
| large | must | big | even |
| such | because | turn | here |
| end | ask | went | men |
| need | land | why | read |
| try | home | | |
| | move | different | |

# Sport Squish! – D

| picture | | learn | |
| should | | page | |

| air | again | still | animal |
| play | woman | letter | away |
| go | change | study | point |
| spell | world | mother | house |

| off | found | |
| high | answer | |

Prim-Ed Publishing — www .prim-ed.com     *Early Literacy Games*     – 42 –

# Desert Squish!

♦ **Aim**

To practise and consolidate sight vocabulary. It is important that the players find it to be a positive and enjoyable experience. This promotes self-esteem.

♦ **Equipment Needed**

- Die with numbers 1 – 6.
- Four sets of different coloured counters (with four in each set).
- Game board A, B, C or D. (Each game board has different words chosen from the 300 commonly used words list.)

♦ **How to Play**

- Number of players – 2 to 4

- Each player decides which camel driver they will be – number 3,8,1 or 7. He/she then places his/her four same coloured counters on the camels near their driver.

- The aim is to ensure the driver safely herds each of his/her four camels to the opposite side of the game board.

- The camel drivers move the camels in turn, by throwing a die and moving the corresponding number on the die. According to the abilities of the children playing, the camels could move in different ways:

Level 1 –  Camels can only move forwards, in straight lines across the board. Camels may not move backwards, sideways or diagonally.

Level 2 –  Camels can move forwards, backwards and sideways but not diagonally.

- Along the way, there are oases at which to rest and drink. If a driver lands on an oasis he/she may take a drink by reading the word. If a driver cannot read a word tell them the word and ask them to look at it and repeat it.

- If a 'camel' lands on an opponent's 'camel', the opponent is 'squished' and sent back to start the journey again.

- More than one 'camel' can be crossing at the same time.

- The game ends when all the camel drivers safely herd all their camels to the opposite side of the game board.

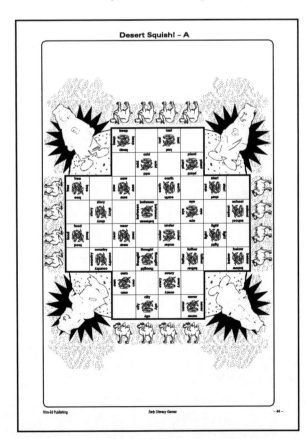

# Desert Squish! – A

# Desert Squish! – B

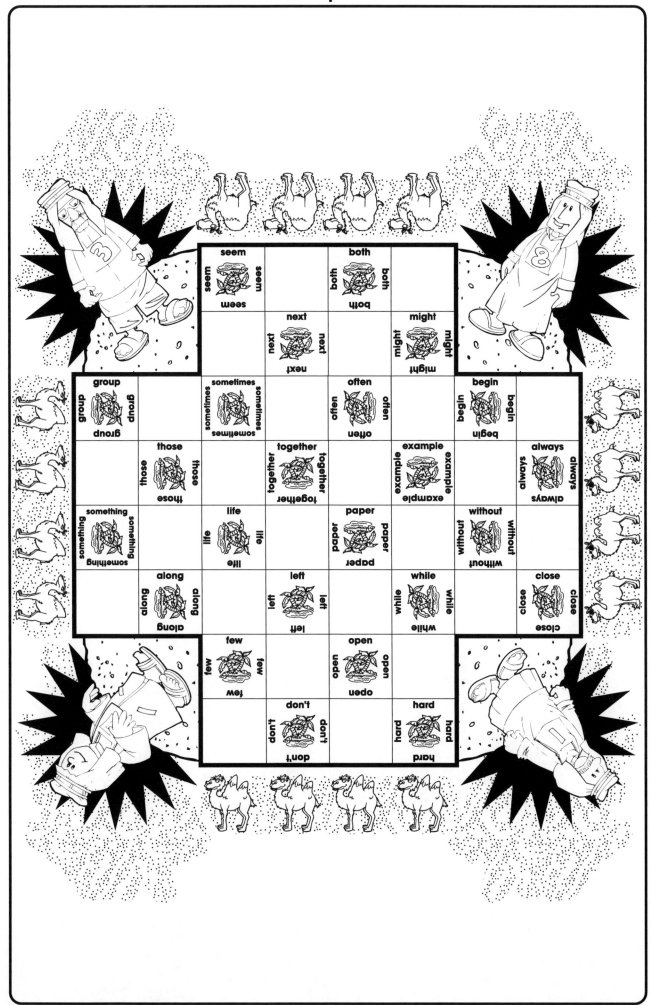

*Early Literacy Games*

# Desert Squish! – D

*Early Literacy Games*

# Common Words – First Hundred

| | | | | |
|---|---|---|---|---|
| the **1** | be **1** | an **1** | make **1** | been **1** |
| of **2** | this **2** | each **2** | like **2** | call **2** |
| and **3** | have **3** | which **3** | him **3** | who **3** |
| a **1** | from **1** | she **1** | into **1** | oil **1** |
| to **2** | or **2** | do **2** | time **2** | now **2** |
| in **3** | one **3** | how **3** | has **3** | find **3** |
| is **1** | had **1** | their **1** | look **1** | long **1** |
| you **2** | by **2** | if **2** | two **2** | down **2** |
| that **3** | word **3** | will **3** | more **3** | day **3** |
| it **1** | but **1** | up **1** | write **1** | did **1** |

Note: The numbers 1, 2 or 3 on each card refer to the number of spaces the player will move in the game.

# Common Words – First Hundred

| | | | | |
|---|---|---|---|---|
| he **2** | not **2** | other **2** | go **2** | get **2** |
| was **3** | what **3** | about **3** | see **3** | come **3** |
| for **1** | all **1** | out **1** | number **1** | made **1** |
| on **2** | were **2** | many **2** | no **2** | may **2** |
| are **3** | we **3** | then **3** | way **3** | part **3** |
| as **1** | when **1** | them **1** | could **1** | over **1** |
| with **2** | your **2** | these **2** | people **2** | his **2** |
| can **3** | so **3** | my **3** | they **3** | said **3** |
| some **1** | than **1** | I **1** | there **1** | her **1** |
| first **2** | at **2** | use **2** | would **2** | water **2** |

Note: The numbers 1, 2 or 3 on each card refer to the number of spaces the player will move in the game.

# Common Words – Second Hundred

| | | | | |
|---|---|---|---|---|
| new **1** | sentence **1** | want **1** | why **1** | away **1** |
| sound **2** | man **2** | show **2** | ask **2** | animal **2** |
| take **3** | think **3** | also **3** | went **3** | house **3** |
| only **1** | say **1** | around **1** | men **1** | point **1** |
| little **2** | great **2** | form **2** | read **2** | page **2** |
| work **3** | where **3** | three **3** | need **3** | letter **3** |
| know **1** | help **1** | small **1** | land **1** | mother **1** |
| place **2** | through **2** | set **2** | different **2** | answer **2** |
| year **3** | much **3** | put **3** | home **3** | found **3** |
| live **1** | before **1** | end **1** | us **1** | study **1** |

Note: The numbers 1, 2 or 3 on each card refer to the number of spaces the player will move in the game.

# Common Words – Second Hundred

| | | | | |
|---|---|---|---|---|
| me 2 | line 2 | does 2 | move 2 | still 2 |
| back 3 | right 3 | another 3 | try 3 | learn 3 |
| give 1 | too 1 | well 1 | kind 1 | should 1 |
| most 2 | mean 2 | large 2 | hand 2 | sleep 2 |
| very 3 | old 3 | must 3 | picture 3 | world 3 |
| after 1 | any 1 | big 1 | again 1 | high 1 |
| thing 2 | same 2 | even 2 | change 2 | our 2 |
| tell 3 | such 3 | off 3 | just 3 | boy 3 |
| because 1 | play 1 | name 1 | follow 1 | turn 1 |
| spell 2 | good 2 | came 2 | here 2 | air 2 |

Note: The numbers 1, 2 or 3 on each card refer to the number of spaces the player will move in the game.

# Common Words – Third Hundred

| | | | | |
|---|---|---|---|---|
| every ❶ | head ❶ | both ❶ | river ❶ | let ❶ |
| near ❷ | under ❷ | paper ❷ | four ❷ | above ❷ |
| add ❸ | story ❸ | together ❸ | carry ❸ | girl ❸ |
| food ❶ | saw ❶ | sometimes ❶ | state ❶ | got ❶ |
| between ❷ | left ❷ | group ❷ | once ❷ | side ❷ |
| own ❸ | don't ❸ | often ❸ | book ❸ | cut ❸ |
| below ❶ | few ❶ | without ❶ | here ❶ | young ❶ |
| country ❷ | while ❷ | important ❷ | stop ❷ | talk ❷ |
| plant ❸ | along ❸ | until ❸ | run ❸ | seen ❸ |
| last ❶ | might ❶ | children ❶ | second ❶ | list ❶ |

Note: The numbers 1, 2 or 3 on each card refer to the number of spaces the player will move in the game.

# Common Words – Third Hundred

| | | | | |
|---|---|---|---|---|
| school **2** | close **2** | mountain **2** | late **2** | song **2** |
| father **3** | something **3** | feet **3** | miss **3** | leave **3** |
| keep **1** | seem **1** | enough **1** | idea **1** | family **1** |
| tree **2** | next **2** | mile **2** | car **2** | body **2** |
| never **3** | hard **3** | night **3** | eat **3** | music **3** |
| start **1** | open **1** | walk **1** | face **1** | colour **1** |
| city **2** | example **2** | white **2** | watch **2** | earth **2** |
| begin **3** | sea **3** | far **3** | eye **3** | life **3** |
| began **1** | woman **1** | light **1** | always **1** | grow **1** |
| real **2** | thought **2** | those **2** | took **2** | almost **2** |

Note: The numbers 1, 2 or 3 on each card refer to the number of spaces the player will move in the game.

# Onset Sounds

| | | | | |
|---|---|---|---|---|
| b | v | cr | sp | kn |
| b | h | dr | sp | thr |
| c | h | dr | ch | thr |
| c | g | fl | ch | br |
| ch | gr | fl | ab | br |
| ch | gr | sm | ab | cl |
| f | l | sm | thr | cl |
| f | l | sh | thr | bl |
| m | st | sh | tr | bl |
| m | st | pr | tr | gr |

# Onset Sounds

| | | | | |
|---|---|---|---|---|
| s | d | pr | bl | gr |
| s | d | spr | bl | sn |
| r | gl | spr | gr | sn |
| r | gl | tr | gr | th |
| w | tr | qu | th | w |
| wh | qu | n | j | wh |
| bl | n | j | y | bl |
| p | t | y | fl | p |
| t | fr | fl | v | cr |
| fr | kn | | | |

# Rime Sounds

| | | | | |
|---|---|---|---|---|
| at | or | old | own | at |
| all | old | ock | an | all |
| ill | ock | an | ell | ill |
| ice | and | ell | out | ice |
| and | ay | out | ow | ate |
| ay | ee | ow | ate | en |
| ee | ake | ad | en | e |
| ake | ad | ear | e | ame |
| ig | ear | op | ame | ig |
| eat | op | ar | eat | ack |

# Rime Sounds

| | | | | |
|---|---|---|---|---|
| ar | end | ack | un | end |
| een | un | et | een | y |
| et | ew | y | ot | ew |
| o | ot | id | o | ow |
| id | or | ow | own | |

# Beginnings

| | | | | |
|---|---|---|---|---|
| ba | be | bi | bo | bu |
| ca | co | cu | da | de |
| do | du | di | fa | fe |
| fi | fo | fu | ga | ha |

# Beginnings

| | | | | |
|---|---|---|---|---|
| he | hi | ho | hu | ja |
| je | ji | jo | ju | la |
| le | li | lo | ma | me |
| mi | mo | mu | na | ne |
| ni | no | nu | pa | pe |
| pi | po | ra | ri | ro |
| ru | sa | se | si | so |
| su | ta | te | ti | to |
| tu | va | wa | we | wi |
| wu | ye | zi | | |

**Note: wa as in wall**

# Endings

| | | | | |
|---|---|---|---|---|
| b | b | ck | ck | d |
| d | ff | ff | g | g |
| ll | ll | m | m | n |
| n | p | p | r | r |
| s | s | ss | ss | t |
| t | x | x | zz | |

## Scoresheet

**Name:**

### Words Made

## Scoresheet

**Name:**

### Words Made

**Name:**

**Name:**

# Word Card Master Sheet

# Reception Year

The words below are essential high frequency words which pupils will need to recognise to be able to read simple texts. The words need to be reinforced through a variety of activities, so pupils are able to read them both in and out of context. By the end of the Reception year, pupils should be able to read all of the following words.

| | | | |
|---|---|---|---|
| I | go | come | went |
| up | you | day | was |
| look | are | the | of |
| we | this | dog | me |
| like | going | big | she |
| and | they | my | see |
| on | away | mum | it |
| at | play | no | yes |
| for | a | dad | can |
| he | am | all | |
| is | cat | get | |
| said | to | in | |

# Years 1 and 2

The words below are essential high frequency words which pupils will need to recognise to be able to read simple texts. The words need to be reinforced through a variety of activities, so pupils are able to read them both in and out of context. By the end of the Year 2, pupils should be able to read all of the following words.

| | | |
|---|---|---|
| about | jump | their |
| after | just | them |
| again | last | then |
| an | laugh | there |
| another | little | these |
| as | live(d) | three |
| back | love | time |
| ball | made | too |
| be | make | took |
| because | man | tree |
| bed | many | two |
| been | may | us |
| boy | more | very |
| brother | much | want |
| but | must | water |
| by | name | way |
| call(ed) | new | were |
| came | next | what |
| can't | night | when |
| could | not | where |
| did | now | who |
| do | off | will |
| don't | old | with |
| dig | once | would |
| door | one | your |
| down | or | |
| first | our | Plus: |
| from | out | • days of the week; |
| girl | over | • months of the year; |
| good | people | • numbers to twenty; |
| got | push | • common colour words |
| had | pull | • blue |
| half | put | • green |
| has | ran | • yellow |
| have | saw | • orange |
| help | school | • red |
| her | seen | • white |
| here | should | • black |
| him | sister | • brown |
| his | so | • pink |
| home | some | • purple |
| house | take | |
| how | than | |
| if | that | |